21 Days of Fasting & Prayer to deal with stubborn situations- Charles Magaiza Snr

Title: **CASTING DOWN STRONGHOLDS**

Copyright (c) 2017 Purpose Clinic Publishing:

Tel: +27719022715

Email: admin@purposeclinic.com

Purpose Clinic books and materials maybe purchased for educational, business, or sales promotional use. Online Editions are also available for most titles. For more information, contact our sales department: admin@purposeclinic.com

ISBN: 978-1-920664-38-1

All scripture quotations are from the King James Version unless it is stated.

INTRODUCTION

CASTING DOWN STRONGHOLDS~ 21 DAYS OF FASTING AND PRAYER TO DEAL WITH STUBBORN SITUATIONS.

About this devotional

This devotional is intended to guide you in your fasting and prayer to pull down a type of resistant strongholds. The words are meant to encourage you to continue despite the devil's attempt to fight you so you can stop going ahead. You need to understand that the battle is not in the physical realm but in the spiritual realm. Have struggled with a disease that won't go away? An addiction, depression or a troublesome marriage? There are many of these areas where the enemy puts his grip and resists many methods of spiritual counter attack. This devotional addresses that.

Ephesians 6:12 (Living Bible)

For we are not fighting against people made of flesh and blood, but against persons without bodies—the evil rulers of the unseen world, those mighty satanic beings and great evil princes of darkness who rule this world; and against huge numbers of wicked spirits in the spirit world.

The Living Bible makes this verse easy to understand. There are demons out there and they are persons without bodies. Evil spirit looking for an opportunity to derail your life at the least opportunity. But do not fear because the greater work was done by Christ on the cross, they were defeated! They now operate through deception. Which is why a program like this one should empower you to win any form battle.

The enemy is real and we should therefore not be ignorant of the reality. Ignorance is not an excuse!

Psalms 74:20 (AMP)

Have regard for the covenant [You made with Abraham], for the dark places of the land are full of the habitations of violence.

This devotional with the prayers and declarations should help you claim your position in Christ and to re-establish the hedge of spiritual protection around you. It doesn't matter your background, with the guidance of the Holy Spirit you will make progress as you go through the period of prayer and fasting.

Prayer and fasting

One of the major keys to unlocking a stubborn situation is prayer combined with fasting. This is a mystery we see both in the New and Old Testament. Jesus Christ uncaps this when He comes down the mountain and his disciples had been approached by a man whose child had a demon. This type of spirit was stubborn and sometimes through the child into water or fire. It was after total destruction of his life. The disciples had tried everything but in vain. When Jesus comes down from the mountain, he rebuked the spirit at the begging of the father and it left the child.

In private, the disciples wanted to know and understand why they could not cast out the evil spirit? They were good students who wanted to correct their mistakes and do better next time. Jesus answered them;

Matthew 17:20-21 (KJV)

And Jesus said unto them, Because of your unbelief: for verily I say unto you, If ye have faith as a grain of mustard seed, ye shall say unto this mountain, Remove hence to yonder place; and it shall remove; and nothing shall be impossible unto you. Howbeit this kind goeth not out but by prayer and fasting.

His response is deep and I would like us to look intently at it but then end up at the core of what we are dealing with (verse 21)

Matthew 17:21 (KJV)

Howbeit this kind goeth not out but by prayer and fasting.

Let's look at it from the Amplified Version,

Matthew 17:20-21

He said to them, Because of the littleness of your faith [that is, your lack of firmly relying trust]. For truly I say to you, if you have faith [that is living] like a grain of mustard seed, you can say to this mountain, Move from here to yonder place, and it will move; and nothing will be impossible to you.

But this kind does not go out except by prayer and fasting.

Lack of faith

Jesus attributed their failure to deal with the evil spirit to a lack of faith and He goes on to reveal that faith as small as a mustard seed is capable of moving mountains. "You can say to this mountain move from here to younder place and it will move, and nothing will be impossible to you." So Christ gives this as the number one solution to moving a stubborn stronghold.

Someone maybe asking how do I get faith? If you are born again, you already have been given a measure of faith upon your salvation.

Romans 12:3 (KJV)

For I say, through the grace given unto me, to every man that is among you, not to think of himself more highly than he ought to think; but to think soberly, according as God hath dealt to every man the measure of faith.

So there is the measure of faith that has been 'dealt' to every man which can be interpreted as something that every believer has. As a child of God, do not look down upon yourself and say 'I don't have the faith to deal with what I am facing!' You do have a measure given and if faith as small as a grain of mustard seed can move mountains, then what you have is capable of doing much!

Let us define a stronghold

I am sure we all understand that the experiences we have originate from the spiritual realm. The story of Job reveals a lot about the source of adversity including loss, disease, premature death, depression and many other negatives. It was the devil behind all the calamity (Job 1:12). In the same way, all good gifts are from above. God is the giver of good gifts (Matthew 7:11).

A stronghold is a satanic siege which is harder to break. It is like the city of Jericho which was described in Joshua 6:1 as **" Now Jericho was straitly shut up because of the children of Israel: none went out, and none came in."** The deep seated demon would have taken charge, often a principality and will be ushering in all sorts of attacks. It can manifest as a disease, financial situation, barrenness, spiritual husbands, addiction or any form of situation difficult to break. Nothing in and nothing out! These are strong words which describe a siege. Some of these result from the fact the evil spirit has been in possession for long it refuses to let go. Some are a result of familiar spirits operating in the family for ages and hence have become generational curses. They will need a different approach to break their hold.

A stronghold is therefore any situation that is resisting ordinary prayer. Answers seem to prolong even though you pray about it often. Some of these come through impartation through laying on of hands. Be careful who you trust with your spiritual walk.

This kind

Christ indicates there are different kinds of evil spirits and this kind (stronghold) needed a different approach which is prayer and fasting;

Matthew 17:21 (KJV)

Howbeit this kind goeth not out but by prayer and fasting.

It has tied itself in and is resistant until one triggers prayer combined with fasting! It gives your spiritual man the impetus and level of faith to get the evil spirit to detach itself. This could be from yourself or a loved one or another person that you are praying for who is tormented by the devil. Faith always remains at the centre of the whole approach. Look at how the walls of Jericho fell according to Hebrews 11:30;

"By faith the walls of Jericho fell down, after they were compassed about seven days."

For seven days Joshua and his people had to be resolute knowing they were not dealing with simple instruction. They needed to adhere to God's command and exercise faith of a higher degree for those walls to fall! With obedience to what God had said, they received their desired result. You child of God must not give up!

There is a way out of your situation and now when you are ready, we let us embark on the twenty one days journey.

CASTING DOWN STRONGHOLDS~ DAY 1 FAST & PRAYER

The word 'strongholds' is often used in Christian circles but rarely do we define what we mean by it. I have found the book of Joshua as a great picture of casting down strongholds and hopefully over the next few days, we can break down the word and be able to pray with direction in terms of what we must deal with during this corporate or individual prayer and fasting.

My definition of a stronghold is 'a defence system that the enemy has put in place to keep the children of God away from their promises.' Now this might sound simple to the ear but a deeper meditation of the words can reveal a lot of things. The children of Israel dealt with physical strongholds (things they could see) but on this side of the Calvary, we often deal with spiritual ones (in hiding). We will go deeper on this.

Joshua 6:10 (AMP)

But Joshua commanded the people, you shall not shout or let your voice be heard, nor shall any word proceed out of your mouth until the day I tell you to shout. Then you shall shout!

One of the key things that I need you to grasp today is the word OBEDIENCE and control of your tongue. The words that you speak are powerful beyond measure and have the capacity of bringing your promises to nothing. One might be wondering why their prayers are not receiving answers, examine your words, do you speak in line with God's word or you just utter things that come into your head?

The walls of Jericho fell because the children of Israel obeyed Joshua who in turn was speaking the word that God had given him. They were quiet when they needed to be quiet and opened their mouths when they shouted upon being asked to. Many lose their blessing through murmuring. The voices of the children of Israel buttered the walls of Jericho and they fell flat. Consider the words of Solomon:

Proverbs 10:19 (AMP)

In a multitude of words transgression is not lacking, but he who restrains his lips is prudent.

It is very important that you control your tongue! There are some things that must not be spoken by your lips as there are spiritual beings ready to act on them, your voice is like a signature. Do you know that your voice is unique as your finger prints? Institutions like banks now are putting systems in place in which are called 'voice recognition' when you call the systems will recognize your voice and they will not need to do all the checks they used to do in the past. Today as you pray, decide to sign what you must sign with your voice.

Cast away sin! OBEDIENCE to God's word is key. Obey His voice and His command. Don't let sin take over your life again otherwise your salvation is just an invalid story. There are things the Holy Spirit will speak in your heart (inner man), don't delay to obey! Be quick as that will ensure strongholds fall:

Prayer Points for Today:

✓Seek out areas of disobedience and confess and repent over them. Any area of sin

✓Seek out areas where your mouth was a free agent and decide to harness your tongue, only speak as God speaks. This means you have to speak in line with God's word.

✓Build your faith strong by reading the word, surely a miracle must take place in these 21 days. Your victory is certain. The word of God is the seed of any miracle, all things were created by His word.

CASTING DOWN STRONGHOLDS ~DAY 2 FAST & PRAYER

Yesterday we laid the foundation of the key things we need to do in casting down strongholds. We realized that obedience to God and our voice (the things we speak) are key to our success in this journey. The book of Joshua stands out for us as part of this great feat. The children of Israel needed no battering rams and natural weapons to bring down the walls of Jericho as they obeyed and acted on the word, using their voices according to God's word wonderful miracles took place on their behalf.

I mentioned that on this side of the Calvary, we are dealing with enemies that we can't see. Let's go to the book of Ephesians:

Ephesians 6:12 (AMP)

For we are not wrestling with flesh and blood [contending only with physical opponents], but against the despotisms, against the powers, against [the master spirits who are] the world rulers of this present darkness, against the spirit forces of wickedness in the heavenly (supernatural) sphere.

One of the key things to note here is that we are 'wrestling!' This is by any measure one of the most intense fight. Wrestling is something I do not allow my children to watch owing to the violence. Apostle Paul says we are not engaged in this against flesh and blood, not only with physical opponents but a highly organized satanic kingdom which is presiding over this present darkness. He points there are the world rulers. In other words, all those that don't belong to Christ are under this kingdom's control. Let's look at the Living Bible translation:

Ephesians 6:12Living Bible (TLB)

12 For we are not fighting against people made of flesh and blood, but against persons without bodies—the evil rulers of the unseen world, those mighty satanic beings and great evil princes of darkness who rule this world; and against huge numbers of wicked spirits in the spirit world.

This translation calls the demons persons without bodies. They are seeking expression! When Jesus cast them out of a man, they were willing to go into pigs. You have to stand guard, don't be imprudent on things, as these persons are seeking a door through which they can attack you. They have been around many years and know your blood line beyond your own knowledge. I am not here to ignite fear, we have the Holy Spirit as a Helper! The key is to obey and listen to His leadership!

Most of the problems you are facing originate here (spiritual realm) not in the natural. Before you blame your neighbour for your challenges, deal with the spiritual.

Luke 10:19 (KJV)

Behold, I give unto you power to tread on serpents and scorpions, and over all the power of the enemy: and nothing shall by any means hurt you.

In closing don't be afraid, power has been given to you. With the Holy Spirit in you, you are empowered to chase thousands of demons.

PRAYER POINTS FOR TODAY

✓Examine possible points where the enemy might have gained entry and control. Is it a repeated sin despite repentance?

✓Are you battling an uncontrolled area of your life which seem to refuse your harness? Pray for deliverance from another being finding expression through you.

✓Denounce the power of the enemy over you as you declare the total Lordship of Jesus Christ over your life.

✓Renounce any area in which the devil might use to lay claim over your life: the occult comes to mind. Things you were made to do as a child or you did as a grown up i.e. going to witch doctors, blood sacrifices, trying to evoke spirits of the dead etc.

✓Search your home, are there objects linking you to the devil? If any found burn them. Ask the Holy Spirit to reveal things to you. It could be paintings, books, artefacts and other things. Tomorrow we will go deeper as we cast down strongholds!

CASTING DOWN STRONGHOLDS~ DAY 3 FAST & PRAYER

So here we go again, the walls of Jericho fell through obedience and the power of the voices of the children of Israel. Yesterday we saw how we are in a wrestling match against an invisible spiritual world. Some try to negotiate with this world system by trying to conform to it through the occult, appeasing the demonic spirits. One must however know that the devil wants your soul in one place and that is in hell. He honours no contract and respects no offering made to him. He is cunning and father of all lies.

It is imperative that you grow up spiritually because the longer you stay a spiritual baby, the longer you keep yourself exposed to attacks of all sorts from the evil kingdom.

1 Corinthians 3:1-2 (KJV)

And I, brethren, could not speak unto you as unto spiritual, but as unto carnal, even as unto babes in Christ. I have fed you with milk, and not with meat: for hitherto ye were not able to bear it, neither yet now are ye able.

The Apostle here is addressing brethren and not heathens. He says at their age (spiritual maturity) they would have been meat eaters but he kept feeding them milk. They could not bear it. They had not made the move from carnality into spirituality. The one who is grown interprets things spiritually but the one who is a baby sees everything with natural eyes. No discernment on their part of spiritual things!

Brethren, strongholds will not fall for the carnal! The devil and his cohorts will be laughing. Decide today to go to the level of a grown up, a spiritual meat eater! Not a baby needing milk. Envying, strife and divisions are all named under carnality. Are you one who occupies yourself envying what others have, striving with your husband or wife and causing divisions amongst the brethren? You are on milk, examine yourself! Time to move up! Break those internal strongholds first and you will see the outside ones fall!

So one can be in church and be carnally driven opening massive doors to the operation of the devil! Cut ties with carnality. Babies touch anything and they put in their mouth. Take your eyes off pornographic materials, sleeping around even though you call yourself a believer, stealing and many other ways of living. Turn around! Changing girlfriends every month after breaking their hearts and using them, you are on milk! Be careful a demon will hi jack your life style!

TODAY'S PRAYER POINTS:

✓Leave carnality and choose to grow in the things of God. Milk is fit for babies, choose spiritual meat.

✓Repent for carnality you might have engaged in. Please note that we are still laying the foundation because purity is important in this battle.

✓Without holiness no man can see God, work on your relationship with God.

✓Continue dealing (praying against) the persons without bodies (demons) assigned against your life.

✓Those familiar spirits that have been tracking your life must meet their demise during this fast season. They must and they will fall! You have the blood of Jesus on your side shed for your victory.

CASTING DOWN STRONGHOLDS ~ DAY 4 FAST & PRAYER

The children of Israel were very busy on the other side of the Jordan. They were able to take over kingdoms of their enemies because the Lord our God was with them. Today I want you to know that with our God, nothing is impossible! As long as we stand with Him on His side, despite every attack the enemy mounts, we are the ones that emerge victorious.

Joshua was now an old man and his personal mission was coming to an end:

Joshua 23:14 (AMP)

And behold, this day I am going the way of all the earth. Know in all your hearts and in all your souls that not one thing has failed of all the good things which the Lord your God promised concerning you. All have come to pass for you; not one thing of them has failed.

These words stirred my spirit concerning the faithfulness of God. Joshua says, 'not ONE thing has failed of all the GOOD things which the Lord your God promised concerning you. ALL have come to pass; not ONE thing has failed.' God's promises are YES and AMEN in Christ Jesus. Strongholds will fall because God said so! It doesn't matter what your enemies are doing to try and bring you down, you will rise again! Your later end will be greater to the embarrassment of those who chant your name for the wrong reasons. See these words from Joshua;

Joshua 23:10 (AMP)

One man of you shall chase a thousand: for the Lord your God, he it is that fighteth for you, as he hath promised you.

Who fights for you? The Lord your God as He promised. As a result you can chase a thousand! The battle is not yours but the Lord's! When He fights for you, your enemies are sure to melt! I want you to continually keep in mind Ephesians 6. Our enemies are not physical! We are fighting persons without bodies. Awaken to this reality, the problem is not your wife or husband; the problem is not your aunt or the in laws. It is demonic forces seeking expression through different individuals. But today hold fort and stand on the promises, let God arise and scatter His enemies!

When they came to arrest Jesus, one of the disciples attacked someone with a sword. Though in grief Jesus wanted the scriptures to be fulfilled and He spoke to the disciple;

Matthew 26:53 (AMP)

Do you suppose that I cannot appeal to My Father, and He will immediately provide Me with more than twelve legions [more than 80,000] of angels?

More than 80,000 angels were at his disposal at His call but He would not make the call because the mission of redemption (moving power from the devil would not be fulfilled). He willingly went through it for scriptures to be fulfilled in your life!

I said strongholds must fall today because He went through it so you don't have to. He wanted these promises to take effect in your life! Strongholds must fall because that spells the fulfilment of scriptures. Every promise must come to pass, every one of them! Not a single one should fail. The enemy must know today that he has targeted the wrong person! At your call the Father can deploy more than 80,000 angels, just to ensure the scriptures are fulfilled! All of the promises: health, finances, protection, joy, satisfactory life, long life and many more to mention. Not a single one should fall short. Know your rights as a born again child of God!

TODAY'S PRAYER POINTS

✓Claim all promises, none should fail to be fulfilled. Identify scriptures in the word that are in line with what you are going through.

✓The other side of the Jordan must signify the other side of the cross, the side we are and here we see promises fulfilled.

✓Know that Satan was defeated on the cross and pray with the knowledge that power is in your hands. He gave you power! Don't pray with fear but with faith.

✓God is with you and on your side, He is your Father, claim protection from all evil.

✓Command the persons without bodies (demons) not to dare touch you because you are under Christ's covering.

✓Refuse any form of bargain or compromise the devil wants to give: every stronghold must fall! Refuse things like 'keep this and I will take that away or take that and I remove this' every stronghold must fall now! It's all deception.

✓All the promises are yours and yes just in case the enemy tries to continue harassing you, Jesus gave you access to more than twelve legions of angels, more than 80,000. Don't be silent call on Him!

CASTING DOWN STRONGHOLDS DAY5 ~ FAST & PRAYER

As one gets into battle, it is important that they are fully equipped. This is important to ensure that you can fight with the right amour on. Here is a bit of reading:

Ephesians 6:14-17 (AMP)

Stand therefore [hold your ground], having tightened the belt of truth around your loins and having put on the breastplate of integrity and of moral rectitude and right standing with God,

And having shod your feet in preparation [to face the enemy with the firm-footed stability, the promptness, and the readiness produced by the good news] of the Gospel of peace.

Lift up over all the [covering] shield of saving faith, upon which you can quench all the flaming missiles of the wicked [one].

And take the helmet of salvation and the sword that the Spirit wields, which is the Word of God.

The key things that are highlighted here are:

1. Belt of truth: this one needs to be tightened around your loins. For the Roman soldier this ensured that all the mid-section was holding and all his weaponry had somewhere to hang. No surprise this receives first mention. Truth is the word of God and one must give truth the highest regard. A determined respect of the truth, no compromise! No stealing, no fornication and adultery, stand in truth in public and in private!

2. Breastplate of integrity and of moral rectitude and right standing with God (righteousness). The breastplate covers a vital part, the heart! It is right standing with God that is going to ensure total protection and moral standing. This you don't have to do anything to achieve, it's a gift from God but you don't abuse it! You have to walk in righteousness all the time.

3. Feet shod with the preparation of the gospel of peace. This gives stability in battle, ready to proclaim the good news or gospel to others even when the devil resists it. It earns you serious kingdom points!

4. Shield of faith. This is one important aspect in the confrontation with the enemy. The Apostle Paul says the shield of faith quenches the fiery darts of the enemy. Your enemy is busy throwing darts of fire, it is the shield of faith that is going to quench the darts so that they don't touch you. Without faith it is impossible to please God. Don't walk in fear, build your faith strong through the word of God.

5. Helmet of salvation. This one protects your mind. The devil would want to take over and control your mind to gain access to your inner man. The helmet of salvation protects you here. With the helmet of salvation protect your mind through meditation of the word. Do not pay attention to the frustrations the devil tries to offload on you making you end up with depression.

6. Sword of the Spirit, which is God's word. This is the offensive weapon you have as a believer, God's word. When Jesus was tempted of the devil after 40 days of fasting, His offensive weapon was the Word. He responded to every attack by saying 'It is written.' Do you know what is written in the word concerning your situation? If there is no word in you it means you are vulnerable to the deceptions of the enemy.

Notice that there is nothing provided for covering the back meaning that there is no retreat, no surrender! It's either you win or you win! If you find yourself lacking in any of these areas, it is going to be impossible for strongholds to fall! You have to be a fully-fledged warrior ready to face the enemy.

When you have everything in place, you can hold your ground against the enemy. No matter the situation, you will be able to resist the devil and he will flee!

TODAY'S PRAYER POINTS

✓Check the six areas above in your life, is everything in place?

✓Are there no presumptuous sins? These violate the breastplate exposing your heart to easy attack by the enemy. You become an easy victim.

✓Discard fear, it is the opposite of faith which happens to be central in blocking fiery darts that Satan and his cohorts are throwing.

✓Pray for courage not to turn back, things are going to heat up and the devil will try and fight back. But in this season he must flee.

✓Equip yourself with the word (sharpen your sword). It is going to be critical for you to be able to answer back and say, 'It is written.' Sunday messages are not going to be enough. Study the word and go deeper with every word preached. Your first listen unfortunately captures less than 15%.

Now that you are equipped, confrontation is inevitable as we dig deeper!

CASTING DOWN STRONGHOLDS ~ DAY 6 FAST & PRAYER

Jesus did not die on the cross for nothing. The devil would like you to stay in the dark where your appreciation of the complete work of the cross is not fully comprehended even though you are born again.

Matthew 28:18-19 AMP)

Jesus approached and, breaking the silence, said to them, All authority (all power of rule) in heaven and on earth has been given to Me.

Go then and make disciples of all the nations, baptizing them into the name of the Father and of the Son and of the Holy Spirit,

The disciples were not sure of the direction to take upon the crucification of Christ but according to promise on the 3rd day, He rose from the dead! When they were in that place of misunderstanding, Jesus approached and broke the silence! I prophesy today that every area where things were silent, Jesus is breaking that silence. Financial silence, no answers, silence in your health, silence where you are trying to break an addiction etc. Answers are coming your way and His voice is opening the deaf ears. May He break all form of silence for you!

He said to them 'All authority (all power of rule) in heaven and on earth has been given to me.' I want you to understand that the devil was holding power of the basis of what Adam had done in the garden through high treason against God. In His death, Jesus stripped the devil of all power of rule in heaven and on earth. This means He has no power at all, all he uses is deception and evil tactics!

When he stripped the devil, at the moment he was still in shock of what he had lost, Jesus passed the power to us His disciples and went and sat at the right hand of the Father.

1 Corinthians 2:7-8 (KJV)

But we speak the wisdom of God in a mystery, even the hidden wisdom, which God ordained before the world unto our glory: Which none of the princes of this world knew: for had they known it, they would not have crucified the Lord of glory,

By a simple error of ignorance, his misrule had come to an end in the same way Adam by a simple error of ignorance he brought great torment to the human race. If the princes of this world had known what the cross was all about, they would not have crucified Christ. His job of deception is now to try and make the work of Calvary of no value in the minds of people through deception. Break down his deception, tell him you are not a fool anymore and you are a fully equipped soldier to deal with his attacks. The power is in your hands to command him to move out of the way!

In the past, those who had no understanding tried to appease these demons and princes with blood. They would ask for goats, cattle, chickens and they would graduate to asking for the blood of people. There are many still living this life in which they appease demons. You don't need to; come fully to Christ and you can experience freedom and authority over these devils. Strongholds fell already on the cross, what you are facing now are fakes that the devil has built. Change your view and you will witness the hand of God in all things.

Your mission should be making disciples of all nations. Bringing to them the same freedom that you have experienced. Instead of wrestling with flesh and blood, bring the good news to them. Know that in every area you are in, the blood of Jesus has brought to you more than you can imagine.

1 Corinthians 2:9-10

But as it is written, Eye hath not seen, nor ear heard, neither have entered into the heart of man, the things which God hath prepared for them that love him. But God hath revealed them unto us by his Spirit: for the Spirit searcheth all things, yea, the deep things of God.

Look at that, whilst eyes and ears were in ignorance of the things God has prepared for those who love Him, the Holy Spirit is on assignment from the Father to reveal these to us. The Spirit searches all things, the deep things of God! There are deep things that you can see when these perceived strongholds fall! There are deep things of God which if the Church beholds, we will focus fully on these deep things and not the confusions the devil tries to cast on us through one confusion after another.

As you pray, search for all the areas where you are deceived and take back your authority. You don't have to carry that demon of deception, you don't have to carry that spirit of infirmity! You can command them to go because all power of rule has been given to you!

TODAY'S PRAYER POINTS

✓Claim back your authority in all areas.

✓The devil has no authority to take you back and forth and feed you on crumbs. You have to sit on that table and feast like the king you are.

✓Refuse to carry that demon of depression, fear and infirmity, cast it out!

✓Refuse to be intimidated because there is nothing Christ didn't pay for on that cross.

✓The power the devil bragged with for centuries was taken back exactly 2016 years ago. It is not fair for the devil for all these years to continue hiding behind the power he doesn't have.

✓Take your stand as a well-equipped soldier for Christ, you don't need to be a pastor, deacon or evangelist, the bulk of the work was done. Just rise in the power of the Holy Spirit and exercise that authority.

✓Allow the Holy Spirit to seek the deep things of God for you. Decide today that as you go deep into His things, you will witness deeper things and be a blessing to your world despite the fact the devil tries to tell you that you are insignificant.

Those strongholds are down, run into the city and gather the spoil! 🏃🏃🏃!

CASTING DOWN STRONGHOLDS~ DAY 7 FAST & PRAYER

As we continue building up on this important prayer and fasting, there are things you need to begin to do prophetically. Actions of faith, doing things as one who has already taken possession. Joshua led the children of Israel in taking cities on the other side of Jordan. Let's look at what happened at Ai;

Joshua 8:18 (AMP)

And the Lord said unto Joshua, Stretch out the spear that is in thy hand toward Ai; for I will give it into thine hand. And Joshua stretched out the spear that he had in his hand toward the city.

There are instructions that the Lord will begin to give you that might seem meaningless but you need to obey His voice. Some of the instructions He will give are prophetic actions that you must take. These might appear vain in the natural realm but carry a lot of significance in the spirit realm. The Lord told Joshua, "Stretch out the spear that is in your hand towards Ai; for I will give it into your hand." In other words, if he didn't obey, it would not happen!

Joshua obeyed and stretched the spear and for sure the Lord faithfully put Ai into his hands with the children of Israel that he led! The victory was amazing and it came with great spoil! Today as you pray, take prophetic actions! With the spear in your hand (sword of the Spirit which is the word of God) point at the cities that you must possess. Is it a child you want? Is it a house? Is it healing? Is it deliverance? Find the relevant scripture and point at it! Declare it and the Lord says I will give that city in your hand.

Don't allow doubt to distract you! Do it with the boldness of one who holds the promises of God! The promises which are true and not vain. He says my word will not return to me void but it will accomplish that which I sent it to do! Through His word, you can take possession of your possessions the enemy had deceitfully stolen. This kind of prophetic actions however need knowledge of God's word. Know the word through reading and meditating on it!

Which cities (promises) must you point at today? Be clear, Joshua pointed at Ai on instruction. He didn't point at the sky or another direction. It is Ai he wanted and precision was important! Be precise with your identification of the scriptures and declare them in faith through the day.

TODAY'S PRAYER POINTS

✓Identify the promises that must be fulfilled in your life today and declare them with your mouth.

✓Pray for *Rhema*, revelation knowledge to give you a full view of what God Has promised.

✓Be confident, He who has promised is faithful to fulfil His words. His word does not return to Him void.

✓As you raise the sword of the Spirit, claim your inheritance. No more poverty and sickness, No more torment from demons and satanic forces.

✓You are a winner as you continue to walk in obedience. Ask the Holy Spirit to continue guiding you and for grace to obey His instructions.

CASTING DOWN STRONGHOLDS ~DAY 8 FAST & PRAYER

EM Bounds, one of the greatest teachers on prayer says, 'One of the greatest revelations in the New Testament concerning the Holy Spirit is that He is our helper in prayer.' This is so true in that we need help, supernatural help to overcome the impediments that the enemy tries to put in our way. Prayer is the key to overcome these and it is powered by the Spirit of God. Need I remind you that we are supernatural beings living in a natural world, the Holy Spirit removes spiritual blindness as He leads.

On this eighty day I want to deal with the covenant that God made with Abraham;

Acts 7:8 (AMP)

And [God] made with Abraham a covenant (an agreement to be religiously observed) of which circumcision was the seal. And under these circumstances [Abraham] became the father of Isaac and circumcised him on the eighth day; and Isaac [did so] when he became the father of Jacob, and Jacob [when each of his sons was born], the twelve patriarchs.

When a male child was born, an indicator for the covenant was circumcision on the eighty day as agreed between Abraham and God. When Joshua led the children Israel across the Jordan, the first thing they did was circumcision of those who had not been circumcised.

Joshua 5:2-3 (KJV)

At that time the Lord said unto Joshua, Make thee sharp knives, and circumcise again the children of Israel the second time. And Joshua made him sharp knives, and circumcised the children of Israel at the hill of the foreskins.

This became a strong signal of the covenant between God and the children of Abraham. But this was just a symbol of what God really intended. What He wanted was not just foreskins but the foreskins of the hearts of the people. A fully surrendered heart to Him is priceless!

Today we have many going around calling themselves Christians but their hearts have not encountered the sharp knife of the Holy Spirit. They go where they want to go and do what they want to do but never obeying the Holy Spirit. They are however happy to put a public performance to show the pretence. Let your heart be dealt with fully by the Holy Spirit!

Deuteronomy 30:6 (AMP)

And the Lord your God will circumcise your hearts and the hearts of your descendants, to love the Lord your God with all your [mind and] heart and with all your being, that you may live.

A circumcised heart results in the love of the Lord with all your mind and heart and all your being. This is the key to a successful Christian life. Today refuse to be a superficial believer but one whose life is wholly given to Him. The early church was able to perform the great spiritual feats because they were filled with the Holy Spirit. Examine Stephen, he had no great title but performed mighty works;

Acts 6:3 (KJV)

Wherefore, brethren, look ye out among you seven men of honest report, full of the Holy Ghost and wisdom, whom we may appoint over this business. Acts 6:8

And Stephen, full of faith and power, did great wonders and miracles among the people.

He was full of the Holy Spirit and wisdom, it resulted in Him being full of faith and power and he did GREAT wonders and miracles among the people! They sought nothing else but a heart fully cut by the Holy Spirit! Resulting in a fullness of God's Spirit.

TODAY'S PRAYER POINTS

✓Ask the Holy Spirit to perform a circumcision on your heart on this eighty day.

✓Ask the Holy Spirit to take over everything concerning you so that your prayers may punch beyond the natural. Surely strongholds must fall but you need the help of the Holy Spirit.

✓Ask the Father to help you with every area in which you were superficial. Life is more than being that, you need to rise above that.

✓We want the wonders and miracles of the early church but these will be so as we convey our lives to God fully. He will not use a compromised vessel. Ask Him to examine all areas not fully surrendered in your life.

CASTING DOWN STRONGHOLDS~ DAY 9 FAST & PRAYER

In High school one of the things we learnt was reactions in science. Certain types of chemicals if mixed produced a certain reaction. One of the things that God hated was when the children of Israel started mixing things, having Him as God and then mixing with other gods. It resulted in His wrath vented against them. The reaction was unbearable, they ended up under oppression from their enemies.

Today, as we cast down strongholds, I want to remind you to take a good look at what you bow down to! Remember the devil is a master of deception and at times he poses as an angel of light. Prudence is important as you observe what you touch, eat, put up in your home etc. Some of you are holding to traditional artefacts passed on from grandparents, get rid of them! You don't want any contact with the occult. Some of you are allowing other people to lay hands on you and you end up with the wrong impartation. The devil sometimes poses as an angel of light and some of the so called man of God in our day are actually used by the devil. Be careful where you go and who you call father.

2 Corinthians 2:11 (KJV)

Lest Satan should get an advantage of us: for we are not ignorant of his devices.

Satan has devices or methods that he uses. Don't be ignorant of them otherwise he will take advantage of you. Take advantage of the grace that is given to you and refuse to mix things. Trust in the Lord wholly. Don't even sponsor things on the other side with your money; that is still participation! On day nine, we are doing a self-introspection as we search out again areas in which we could be mixing things. God is merciful and is ready to deliver you from all oppression. In times when the children of Israel called to God, He sent them a deliverer! I believe this is your time for deliverance from whatever has been holding you down!

Strongholds must fall, you must hold that baby in your hands! You must be restored to perfect health! You must be free from that unholy sex sin bondage. All this is possible with a total commitment to God. He will deliver you even from the worst situation!

Judges 3:9 (KJV)

And when the children of Israel cried unto the Lord, the Lord raised up a deliverer to the children of Israel, who delivered them, even Othniel the son of Kenaz, Caleb's younger brother.

When the children of Israel transgressed they fell in the hands of their enemies as previously said. When they cried to the Lord a deliverer came from Him. Christ Has redeemed us from the curse of the law, go back to Him! Abandon all other gods and He will change your life completely. He is seated at the right hand of the Father ever living to make intercession for us! He is our provided deliverer.

TODAY'S PRAYER POINTS

✓Search out areas where you might be mixing God with other things. Break ties with these. Some of the things might seem innocent, like palm reading, some prophetic movements (judge all prophesy), and even some gifts that you are given by people.

✓Destroy things that might have been passed on to you with obvious linkages in the occult, those who gave their lives to Christ in the book of Acts burnt things from the other side to totally seal their faith in Christ.

✓Which areas do you need to come back to God in repentance? Remember, you have all the control as to what the outcome of this fast will be in your life. I am declaring victory for you as you follow these instructions.

✓Give praise to God for where He has taken us so far. He is the giver of strength in this fast. There are others who would love to abstain from food but they can't because of various situations.

CASTING DOWN STRONGHOLDS~ DAY 10 FAST & PRAYER

Some things can only move or happen if there is persistence. Many lose out on their blessing because they give up too early. As already said, we have an enemy that is waiting to block anything good coming our way. Cry-babies will give up too early and lose on their blessing.

A good example of persistence is found in Genesis as Jacob crossed the brook Jabbok.

Genesis 32:24-28 (AMP)

And Jacob was left alone, and a Man wrestled with him until daybreak.

And when [the Man] saw that He did not prevail against [Jacob], He touched the hollow of his thigh; and Jacob's thigh was put out of joint as he wrestled with Him.

Then He said, Let Me go, for day is breaking. But [Jacob] said, I will not let You go unless You declare a blessing upon me.

[The Man] asked him, What is your name? And [in shock of realization, whispering] he said, Jacob [supplanter, schemer, trickster, swindler]!

And He said, Your name shall be called no more Jacob [supplanter], but Israel [contender with God]; for you have contended and have power with God and with men and have prevailed.

This will be clearly interpreted by visualizing Jacob wrestling for his blessing. Amplified put the opponent as The Man, This is not an angel here but a member of the trinity. Jacob held on, until the day was breaking and The Man said, "Let me go for day is breaking." In persistence Jacob said I will not let you go until you declare a blessing on me. He asked, what is your name? He said Jacob! He was told your name shall no more be Jacob but Israel for you have contended with God and with man and prevailed.

Here it is, Jacob was not just wrestling The Man but was wrestling God. The blessing came as a change of name. On day ten, you need to wrestle for your blessing. Push push push! Don't let go until things change. Don't let go until you have a new name or identity from Him. Meaning you can no longer operate the way you did and do things the way you did in the past. Things have to change and for it to be so, persistence is key!

Some strongholds are not going to fall easy, they are strong and have been around for long. They need you to be resolute and challenge them with no going back in your fight. The promises that God gave need you to persist until you see God's hand move in your life. If you don't persist, the blessings and promises will escape you.

Clearly your situation needs a strong hand. That hand is going to be yours as God Has put the promises out for you. Wrestle for your promises until those who see you will see you as a new man!

As you pray today

✓Demand your promises. Mention them to God. Pray in faith until your breakthrough comes.

✓Persistence is key, you might be tempted to give up now but I urge you to rise above the pressures and keep the spiritual focus. This time something will give in.

✓It doesn't matter how old the stronghold is, don't be intimidated, wrestle in prayer and declaration of the word.

✓Address the enemy, remind him that you are not his slave and he must restore double everything he stole from you.

CASTING DOWN STRONGHOLDS ~ DAY 11 FAST & PRAYER

The enemy is a bully, he doesn't play fair. He tries to attack you from every angle. At times his demons find it a pleasure to track your life seeking your point of weakness so they attack. But in this season, we are going to bring it down as we take our authority. It is important that we keep our hearts in place with regards our commitment to Him. See what happened to the children of Israel when they transgressed against God and followed Baal;

Judges 6:3-4 (AMP)

For whenever Israel had sown their seed, the Midianites and the Amalekites and the people of the east came up against them.

They would encamp against them and destroy the crops as far as Gaza and leave no nourishment for Israel, and no ox or sheep or donkey.

Because of sin, they were exposed to the devastation of their enemies. Get rid of all sin. Don't play with sin! Whenever you sow seed the enemy wants to come against you so that he blocks your harvest. He wants to destroy any form of crop that comes from your seed! Some of you have wondered what has happened to the seeds you have sown and every year the devastation of your crop or seed has continued! I am talking about miscarriages of children, loss of definite business and losses of different kinds. You have gone down instead of rising! We are protesting today and saying financial Strongholds must fall! Toil should not be your portion especially if you are a tither.

The Midianites and Amalekites no matter how many they are should bow down to your command as a child of God. The word of God spoken and declared causes havoc in the devil's kingdom. I declare no more toil for you. No more miscarriage of any form. Your seed is falling on good ground in Jesus' name! Every tormenting enemy is meeting his demise today in your life in Jesus' name. Every place where your name is being called out for evil I declare that whatever is said is going back to sender in Jesus' name!

TODAY'S PRAYER POINTS

✓Make sure your obedience is complete, when it is so, the devil will have no room to touch you.

✓Overcome all form of fear and rise above it through total commitment to God.

✓You can rise above every financial stronghold today. Pray that the stronghold of lack and toil falls in your life. This is hinged on obedience to his word (tithing, giving, sowing are key).

✓You have the name of Jesus. Speak it over every situation today. It carries enough power to change things completely in your life.

CASTING DOWN STRONGHOLDS~ Day 12 FAST & PRAYER

Praise is a powerful weapon of warfare and on this twelfth day, we want to use this weapon. There are some doors that only praise unlocks, that just prayer can't open! Despite how tough things may look, today take time to praise Him. The word shows us how powerful praise is both in the Old Testament and the New Testament. Let's look at the OT first;

2 Chronicles 20:21 (AMP)

When he had consulted with the people, he appointed singers to sing to the Lord and praise Him in their holy [priestly] garments as they went out before the army, saying, Give thanks to the Lord, for His mercy and loving-kindness endure forever!

Jehoshaphat and his people were surrounded by their enemies. They were more than them and more powerful than them. The word of the Lord came and said you don't need to fight in this battle. Give it over to God through praise. Singers were appointed to sing praise to the Lord. The result was miraculous. The enemies slaughtered themselves as God intervened in the battle!

In the New Testament, Paul and Silas were arrested and put in prison after being beaten. Instead of being depressed and crying, they started praising God;

Acts 16:25-26 (AMP)

But about midnight, as Paul and Silas were praying and singing hymns of praise to God, and the [other] prisoners were listening to them,

Suddenly there was a great earthquake, so that the very foundations of the prison were shaken; and at once all the doors were opened and everyone's shackles were unfastened.

At midnight, they were praying and singing hymns of praise to God. They were not doing it quietly, other prisoners heard them! The result was glorious, suddenly there was an earthquake so that the very foundations of the prison were shaken. At once all the doors were opened and everyone's shackles were unfastened. Chains were broken!

Today, your midnight will be changed as you open your mouth and sing praises to the Lord. You don't need to be quiet. You don't need to be suppressed! Praise Him in the midnight hour, praise Him whilst in pain, and praise Him whilst in lack. Praise will cause strongholds to fall down flat. You don't need a perfected voice or an instrument to assist you. Just open your own mouth and praise! You will see God rise and fight on your behalf. I see the very foundations of your strongholds shaken on the very foundations!

David says,

Psalms 119:164 (AMP)

Seven times a day and all day long do I praise You because of Your righteous decrees.

The ball is in your court, change things through praise! Let closed doors open suddenly because of your praise. Your time to triumph through praise has come.

TODAY'S PRAYER POINTS

✓Take the seven times a day challenge and praise Him today.

✓Vocalize your praise, not just thinking about it.

✓Lift those hands and praise Him for this very day, this very life and grace on your life.

✓I see your enemies turning against each other as strongholds are falling.

✓Your praise is penetrating strong walls and breaking them down.

CASTING DOWN STRONGHOLDS ~ DAY 13 FAST & PRAYER

You are doing well by being assertive, by now a lot of the small strongholds are down but there are those stubborn ones that want to maintain control because they have been around for long and are comfortable. Remember the man with a legion of demons? The demons were almost defying Jesus. They were saying do not cast out, do not send us out of this region (Mark 5:7-10). They were interested in the region. Part of their familiar territory. They eventually begged Jesus to allow them to go into the hogs.

We are in the second period of this fast and so we need to unseat these familiar spirits. Some of these need direct instruction from the Holy Spirit on how to do it. Which brings me to the subject matter of the day, VISIONS AND DREAMS. Be on the alert in this second bit of the fast. The Lord is going to be speaking clearly through visions and dreams. He will be giving instructions on what to do to deal with some situations.

Acts 10:2-3 (AMP)

A devout man who venerated God and treated Him with reverential obedience, as did all his household; and he gave much alms to the people and prayed continually to God.

About the ninth hour (about 3:00 p.m.) of the day he saw clearly in a vision an angel of God entering and saying to him, Cornelius!

As Cornelius, a captain devoted himself to God in prayer and giving, one day he had the encounter as above with the angel of the Lord. This was a vision, fully alert and God spoke and gave clear instructions.

On the other end Peter was praying and the word says this about him;

Acts 10:10-11 (AMP)

But he became very hungry, and wanted something to eat; and while the meal was being prepared a trance came over him,

And he saw the sky opened and something like a great sheet lowered by the four corners, descending to the earth.

Peter was praying and he fell into a trance and he saw a vision and God speaking to Him again giving instructions. There is a level that is going to require step by step instructions from the Lord to get the strongholds down. The devil is not only a master of deception but is also good at hiding. But this time around they cannot stay in the region of your life, family, loved ones, job etc. We are breaking ties and anything he is holding on to will be revealed in this season of revelation!

Dreams come when you are asleep but don't look down upon them because your spirit is alert. Remember Solomon dreamed, answered in the dream and a spiritual contract was sealed (1 Chronicles 1:7-12) the whole Bible is littered with how God spoke and speaks through dreams. This is a subject for another day. But look at the prophet Joel as he saw the time we are living in;

Joel 2:28 (AMP)

And afterward I will pour out My Spirit upon all flesh; and your sons and your daughters shall prophesy, your old men shall dream dreams, your young men shall see visions.

Do you see the dreams and visions? And of course the prophesy! All these are consistent with a high presence and out pouring of the Holy Spirit. Dreams come with instructions, warnings and are direction giving. This is one area that the world has not understood therefore they attribute in to the subconscious mind.

I want you to be heavily alert now because you are going to have dreams with specific instructions. I am reminded of a deliverance session over someone who had a spirit of sickness and lack of progress constantly bothering them. After being prayed for, they slept and the Lord spoke in a dream, "Throw away those peanuts in your house." These had come as a gift. The moment the person woke up they enquired and I told them to burn the peanuts, the sickness left immediately! The peanuts is something they had already forgotten about as they were too few to cook. The devil will try to conceal some things so that the torment, lack, sickness and confusion continues! But your time for total deliverance has come. Be alert to the instructions that will come in visions and dreams;

TODAY'S PRAYER POINTS

✓Pray for alertness to His voice and the power to interpret dreams and visions coming to you.

✓Pray for the power to take immediate action so that the stronghold falls immediately.

✓Pray that those strongholds that were still holding you breakdown in Jesus' name.

✓Pray for strength to pull the last bit of this fast as the devil would want to fight back but greater is He that is in you than he that is in the world.

✓Claim all the good things that belong to you, don't allow the devil to keep stealing from you. Raise your level of violent prayer!

CASTING DOWN STRONGHOLDS~ DAY 14 FAST & PRAYER

There are different levels of strongholds and demons that we have to deal with and all of them need different levels of power and depth. If you choose to remain a baby, you remain a victim and powerless against some of these evil spirits. It results in no change in your life.

Upon descending from the mountain of transfiguration, Jesus encountered a situation in which His disciples were confronted by a desperate father who had a son with a bad demon. The intention of the evil spirit was to kill the child as it would throw him in water and fire. It had tormented him since he was a child. Jesus cast out the demon that the disciples had failed to. As good students, in private they asked why they could not cast it out.

Mark 9:28-29 (AMP)

And when He had gone indoors, His disciples asked Him privately, Why could not we drive it out? And He replied to them, This kind cannot be driven out by anything but prayer and fasting.

I want you to know that as a born again child of God you have been given power to drive out demons. The disciples asked, why could we not drive it out? The demon had proved itself stubborn to them and defied their commands. This may sound familiar in various situations you may be facing. His response was simple yet deep, 'This kind cannot be driven out by anything but prayer and fasting.'

Prayer has to have a base of sanctification for it to be effective. Holiness is the key to powerful prayers. Fasting has the power of humbling you. One man said fasting moves you not God! It humbles you to a level where you can clearly hear God without pride and prejudice. In this time of fasting, make sure your life is being worked on by this fast. Challenge yourself to pray like you have not done before. It is possible to lift your level to over seven hours a day, the question is are you willing? There are strongholds that crumble at a certain level of prayer and fasting! There are also strongholds that are unmoved by a certain level of prayer and fasting!

The spirit of slumber is what tries to make you prayer less and cause you to fail to deal with some marauding demons. You must overcome this spirit. It is easy for you to watch TV for hours without sleeping but the moment you start praying or touch your Bible, you already start sleeping! Today deal with this spirit and rise to a new level in which you command these stubborn spirits with enough authority and power.

TODAY'S PRAYER POINTS

✓There is a demonic siege you must break but it will take more determination in your prayer and fasting. Pray for more determination.

✓Be aware that there is a kind or level of demons that need deeper levels of prayer and fasting. Pray that the Holy Spirit bring you to those levels.

✓Let this time of prayer and fasting be a time that humbles you so that you emerge a better person than you were before.

✓Keep pushing, your change is here, this is a season of answered prayers.

CASTING DOWN STRONGHOLDS ~ DAY 15 FAST & PRAYER

No one can dominate what he doesn't despise! You need to despise the strongholds in your life in order to overcome them. They must know they are under your feet. The enemy needs to know that he is under your feet for him to obey your commands. Revelation and knowledge is key to your victory. Strongholds must fall but knowledge is important!

2 Peter 1:3 (AMP)

For His divine power has bestowed upon us all things that [are requisite and suited] to life and godliness, through the [full, personal] knowledge of Him Who called us by and to His own glory and excellence (virtue).

His divine power has bestowed upon us ALL things that are requisite and suited to life and godliness! This is possible through the full and personal knowledge of Him who called us by His own glory and excellence. This knowledge is personal, not that of your pastor or prophet.

His divine power is real! Understand that all things that pertain to life and godliness have been given to you. How do you receive something given to you? You have to take it by force! There is a devil that is blocking you from receiving your blessing. The word *katalambano* means taking by force. Don't expect the blessing to just land in your hands, fight for it. Be diligent about it and you will be a partaker of these good things.

God doesn't want you to struggle in your life. He wants you to excel in the things of this life and He wants you to excel in godliness. But don't be a baby waiting to be fed, the violent take their inheritance by force. Arise in this season and don't give up! It might look like it has taken time for your blessing to manifest but develop a new level of violence to receive what's yours.

TODAY'S PRAYER POINTS

✓Know that His divine power has given to you all things that pertain to life and godliness. Pray with violence to surpass the strongholds that were blocking your access to good things.

✓Knowledge remains key, know what belongs to you in Christ. In that state no devil will stop your receiving.

✓Pray that every good thing that was blocked by the enemy be released now~ health, wealth, relationships etc.

✓Give thanks to God for what He has already done and fulfilled in your life in Jesus' name.

CASTING DOWN STRONGHOLDS ~ DAY 16 FAST & PRAYER

Now you must be punching strong! Day sixteen must be significant for you and we are drawing closer to that 21st day. You must have cleared a lot of things in your life to allow a seamless flow of the Holy Spirit. I believe every yoke and curse should not find room to operate in your life. Every curse is removed and every yoke is broken!

Mark 11:24 (AMP)

For this reason I am telling you, whatever you ask for in prayer, believe (trust and be confident) that it is granted to you, and you will [get it].

Jesus here gives us an open Cheque in our prayers. He says whatever you ask for in prayer, you must believe that it be granted to you and you will get it. Now there is no limit to what the Lord can do on your behalf as long as you pray believing. He will answer any type of prayer.

There are however some prayers that quickly move God. Today make a commitment to pray for your local church to grow. Pray for souls in your community to be saved. Pray also for your man and woman of God that the Lord would use them and strengthen them. In the Lord's Prayer, Jesus says for us to pray, "Thy kingdom come." When you show interest in kingdom business, God will show interest in your own business. Pray for the souls around you to be born again. Make it a priority!

The fig tree dried at the command of Jesus, anything that is contrary to God's voice at your command must dry up now in the name of Jesus! Don't take no for an answer! Rise in the power of the Holy Spirit for you have been given power over the works of the enemy. At your word, mountains must move!

Don't let this fast pass in vain, it is an opportunity to bring order in your life. Pray in faith and God's hand will be visible in this hour. Your story must change, position yourself spiritually in faith!

I hear the Lord saying He is launching you to another level. Your spiritual life must move from glory to glory, your health must move from glory to glory. It's time to see His glory. What is not ordained by God from the beginning in your life must not at all gain pre-eminence in your life. Be loosed today, be liberated, be set free and see God's word in action in your life. You are going higher and higher with Jesus' name today.

TODAY'S PRAYER POINTS

✓As you pray today, know that whatever you pray and believe for it will be done for you.

✓Pray for your local church and your leaders to be strengthened and protected from the hand of the enemy.

✓Pray for souls, those not born again to find their way into the church. We want the church worldwide to grow and burst out into different nations.

✓Receive your next level in Jesus' name! That fig tree that is contrary must dry up at your word.

CASTING DOWN STRONGHOLDS~DAY 17 FAST & PRAYER

On day 14 I had a vision of the night as follows:

I was praying to God, "Pour out water on my ground Lord." The ground was dry yet next to my field there was one with thriving mealies and there were springs in between our fields. I drilled the ground and brought out water and started watering the ground assuring everyone with me that the seed that was in the ground will immediately bring forth fruit since it was already planted.

Hosea 6:3 (AMP)

Yes, let us know (recognize, be acquainted with, and understand) Him; let us be zealous to know the Lord [to appreciate, give heed to, and cherish Him]. His going forth is prepared and certain as the dawn, and He will come to us as the [heavy] rain, as the later rain that waters the earth.

A lack of knowledge of the Lord is like a dry ground that even when a seed is planted, it will not bring forth fruit because there is lack of water. The Prophet Hosea says recognize, be acquainted with and understand Him. Develop a new zeal for Him and renew your covenant with Him! He says when this has happened, He will come to us as the heavy rain and the later rain that waters the earth. If the rain does this, the seed is assured of germination.

Today I challenge you to pray for God to pour water on your ground. May you experience the former and later rain on your dry ground! Yes He will give you springs and your life will not be the same again. Prayer is the key to this breakthrough! You need this rain on your business, ministry, health, job and life. This will ensure fruitfulness in your life!

Renew your zeal for the Lord and your harvest will be great. Remember the word, "Seek ye first the kingdom of God and His righteousness and all these things will be added to you." Matthew 6:33. When your passion is in order, your ground will never experience dryness again and your seed will sprout and dominate.

TODAY'S PRAYER POINT

✓Ask the Lord to pour water on your dry ground.

✓Renew your zeal for the things of God.

✓Develop your knowledge of God, go deeper through study of the word.

✓The later and the former rain is falling on your ground in Jesus' name.

✓Things must change in your life on this mountain of prayer.

CASTING DOWN STRONGHOLDS ~ DAY 18 FAST & PRAYER

Samson was a miracle child who was announced by an angel and born by a woman who was called barren. He was going to be deliverer of Israel from the grip and oppression of the Philistines.

Judges 13:25 (KJV)

And the Spirit of the Lord began to move him at times in the camp of Dan between Zorah and Eshtaol.

When Samson grew, the Spirit of the Lord started to take control of him at times. I want you to notice the difference between the old covenant and the new. In the covenant we are in sealed by the blood of Jesus, the Holy Spirit dwells in us. We are called God's temple!

Judges 14:5 (KJV)

Then went Samson down, and his father and his mother, to Timnath, and came to the vineyards of Timnath: and, behold, a young lion roared against him.

The word Timnath means 'your assigned portion.' It is in this place that a young lion roared against Samson. It wanted to upset him and unsettle him from his own assigned portion. I want you to know that the devil will try and resist your taking possession of what has been given to you through redemption on the cross! The word says;

1 Peter 5:8-9 (KJV)

Be sober, be vigilant; because your adversary the devil, as a roaring lion, walketh about, seeking whom he may devour: Whom resist stedfast in the faith, knowing that the same afflictions are accomplished in your brethren that are in the world.

Yes the Holy Spirit is dwelling in you but the Apostle Peter tells us to be sober and vigilant because our enemy the devil as a roaring lion walks about seeking whom he may devour. He is looking for an opportunity to unseat you from your God given inheritance. The solution is:

→RESIST HIM

→BE STEADFAST IN THE FAITH

→KNOWLEDGE CONCERNING THE AFFLICTIONS

Samson resisted the young lion and with his bare hands he fought it and tore it apart because of the Spirit of God upon him. You too can do amazing things with the Holy Spirit inside you. Don't let fear take you down, challenge the adversary as he tries to unseat you from your Timnath. Resist him, remain steadfast in the faith, know that there are many other brethren overcoming and have overcome the same afflictions!

TODAY'S PRAYER POINTS

✓Refuse to fear, if you feel the fear, do it anyway.

✓Resist the devil, no matter how much he tries to push you, don't budge.

✓Remain steadfast in faith, no other God, no other solution!

✓Acknowledge the Holy Spirit in you and thank God for the price paid for your redemption on the cross.

✓Your turn to do amazing things in the kingdom has come, the price was paid already on the cross.

CASTING DOWN STRONGHOLDS~ DAY 19 FAST & PRAYER

EW Kenyon a great writer of the past generals wrote, "THERE ARE THREE GREAT WORDS that describe the condition of a believer who is taking advantage of his privileges in Christ- rest, peace, and joy. These three words are the fruit of full-grown faith." These are great words from a great man.

As we are casting down Strongholds, it is important that we get to the stage of full-grown faith. Not to be nursed as babies in the Lord still. Rest, peace and joy are the fruit of those fully grown in faith! Today the challenge is to up your level of prayer and knowledge of God resulting in strong faith which will quench all the fiery darts of the enemy.

3 John 1:2 (AMP)

Beloved, I pray that you may prosper in every way and [that your body] may keep well, even as [I know] your soul keeps well and prospers.

Prosperity is your portion as a child of God, your body must keep well as your soul keeps well. This is your heritage as God's child. Many promises are for grabs for those who rise in Christian maturity.

John 14:27 (AMP)

Peace I leave with you; My [own] peace I now give and bequeath to you. Not as the world gives do I give to you. Do not let your hearts be troubled, neither let them be afraid. [Stop allowing yourselves to be agitated and disturbed; and do not permit yourselves to be fearful and intimidated and cowardly and unsettled.]

We have been given the peace of God, His shalom shalom! Not as the world gives. The commentary that the Amplified version gives is well fitting *[Stop allowing yourselves to be agitated and disturbed; and do not permit yourselves to be fearful and intimidated and cowardly and unsettled.]* failure to accept the peace opens the door for the enemy to operate and frustrate your benefits of redemption.

On this ninetieth day, celebrate the gifts of God in your life. David says;

Psalms 119:164 (AMP)

Seven times a day and all day long do I praise you because of Your righteous decrees.

Lift your hands and praise Him today, victory is imminent. The price was already paid. The benefits of redemption are accruing to you. Every demonic siege is broken today. He who touches you is playing with fire, the one who digs a pit against you will fall into it!

TODAY'S PRAYER POINTS

✓Declare rest, peace and joy in your life being the fruits of matured faith.

✓Give Him praise for praise looks beautiful on you. It unseats any stronghold.

✓Pray in the Spirit, prayer in the Spirit is pleasant to God for we know not what we should pray for on our own but the Holy Spirit leads us well.

✓Take the seven times a day praise challenge again, praise is powerful, it doesn't fail.

✓Claim your peace that surpasses all understanding that the enemy has been trying to steal from you.

CASTING DOWN STRONGHOLDS~ DAY 20 FAST & PRAYER

FF BOSWORTH in one of his books said "If you must doubt anything doubt your doubts." Faith is the foundation of our Christian faith. Without faith it is impossible to please God (Hebrews 11:6). If you must doubt, doubt your own doubts. Don't let the devil get you to start thinking otherwise concerning any matter you are facing. You will win and you will testify no matter how impossible it looks.

I remember in 1996 we went on outreach in rural Mozambique, Africa. We came across a woman who was a well-known witch doctor in the area. We preached Jesus to her and when we started praying for her demons started to manifest. One of the demons started resisting coming out. Upon asking why it was refusing, the answer was, "I brought everything here, the goats, the chickens and all the wealth." You might think goats and chickens are not wealth but we were in a poor community that had just come out of a terrible war. You may also ask why I mention this. The reason is for you to see that there are some strongholds that will need consistent presentation of a SOLID FRONT, no going back or doubting the power you have been given in the name of Jesus!

When you give up on your faith, you give the devil room to operate. The moment doubt moves in, a huge door opens for the enemy to operate unrestricted. You must rise above all doubt. Look to Jesus alone and nothing else!

Matthew 14:28-30 (KJV)

And Peter answered him and said, Lord, if it be thou, bid me come unto thee on the water. And he said, Come. And when Peter was come down out of the ship, he walked on the water, to go to Jesus. But when he saw the wind boisterous, he was afraid; and beginning to sink, he cried, saying, Lord, save me.

At the word of the Lord, Peter disembarked the ship and started walking on the water. Yes he walked on the water just by taking hold of the word of the Master, but something happened as he stood on the word. HE SAW! What are you seeing today? God said to Moses and the children of Israel, "These Egyptians you are seeing today you shall see them no more forever." Exodus 14:13, He first told him to fear not! When Peter saw the wind boisterous, he was AFRAID. The fear opened the door, doubt crept in and he started to sink!

WHAT ARE YOU SEEING TODAY? Are you seeing that disease magnified? Are you seeing yourself sinking lower into that financial situation? What do you see today? Are you seeing that stubborn stronghold refusing to fall? Focus your eyes on Jesus! Declare the name of Jesus without any fear! Even the most stubborn demon will have to leave. That demon in Mozambique left although disgruntled. It might have regained access as the woman didn't also seem to want a change of life.

The word of God is alive. Your situation is not eluding Him. He will fight your battle. He will leap over mountains to bring your deliverance but only faith will move Him. Refuse to fear today, refuse to doubt! If you must doubt, doubt your own doubts.

TODAY'S PRAYER POINTS

✓Refuse to look at the circumstances, look to the Master of life. The one who came to give life in abundance.

✓Don't allow fear to build up in your heart as that is an entrance door for the enemy.

✓Don't doubt the word of God, delay is not denial. That child will come even if you are 50! Be patient.

✓Through faith and patience we shall inherit the promises. Some things need you to give them time, the word of God still works and it will work in your situation.

✓Refuse to look at your situation as something special, there are other believers going through the same and others are already testifying after attaining their victory. You are next in line to testify!

CASTING DOWN STRONGHOLDS~ DAY 21 FAST & PRAYER

Can you believe it? You have made it to the final day of Casting Down Strongholds. The issue I want to raise today is take your possessions by force! They belong to you. Shout, God has given you the city! Power has changed hands and you are in a position to change the whole game plan in your life! Now you know enough not to fear the work of the devil.

I want you to know that you have angels on standby waiting to work at the command of God's word;

Psalms 103:20 (KJV)

Bless the Lord, ye his angels that excel in strength, that do his commandments, hearkening unto the voice of his word.

Angels excel in strength and act at the voice of His word. You now need to vocalize God's word and as you do, Angels will join into this battle to ensure that your victory is certain. Yes without fail God is able to perform wonders!

Today is a day of celebration. A day to rejoice for what He has already fulfilled in the twenty one days. Stand in faith knowing that your enemy has fallen and he now is under your feet. Don't elevate him nor your condition by speaking too much about it. Rather speak his word. Declare your victory in every area where the enemy was fighting you.

Today rise up in your churches and in your homes, sing and dance! You will not fail to see God's hand in a new way from now on. The number twenty one is significant in that Prophet Daniel received his answer on this day. The angel showed up with his answer. Today is your day of answers! It is your day to see the deliverance of the Lord in your situation. Declare your freedom from every binding chain for your time of freedom has come.

I see you rising above challenges! I see you overcoming that trap the enemy had set before you. I see you manifesting as a mature son of God.

Let me take opportunity to declare a turnaround in your business, family, marriage and job! Today you are receiving good news concerning your expectations. I see chains breaking like flax in your hands. Every binding force is meeting its demise today. You are free in Jesus' name! Your family is protected!

If your hands were growing weary and tired, take a new grip with those tired hands. You are about to see God in this season. The flood gates are open and it is raining in your camp! No matter the state of things, believe that the miracle working God has worked miracles on your behalf during this period.

I am happy to see the new you in your new season in which strongholds are not an issue at all!

TODAY'S PRAYER POINTS

✓The main key is to praise the Lord, do it in a new fashion like you have not done before.

✓It is the day to take steps of faith, yes go purchase clothes for that miracle baby because the strongholds have fallen. Do you already have a name for the baby? If not, name the child. Call things that are not as though they were.

✓Continue to speak with and in authority that has been given you. Don't let the devil move you an inch!

✓Release the ministry of angels through the declaration of God's word. The Angels are on standby hearkening to the word of His command. Open your mouth and speak the word and Angels will leap into action.

✓Your future is bright, it will not be hindered by what the devil was trying to do in your life or against you.

CONCLUDING REMARKS

WHEN I CALLED, HE HEARD

For he hath not despised nor abhorred the affliction of the afflicted; neither hath he hid his face from him; but when he cried unto him, he heard. (Psalms 22:24 KJV)

We serve a mighty God, who is capable of hearing and seeing. He is not like dumb idols that others worship. When we go through tough times, He is closer than we can imagine, ready to act upon our call on Him.

The Psalmist says He has not despised nor abhorred the affliction of the afflicted. Are you afflicted in any area? Are you going through a difficult season and you are not sure what to do? His ear is ready to hear you. He will not ignore you, call upon Him! It is His desire to show you His face and grant you victory over marauding demons and the work of the enemy. Call to Him and He will hear you.

Some situations may seem prolonged, you might be losing heart and thinking that there is no way out for you. Let me assure you that there is definitely a way out for you! God's grace is available to ensure that you conquer everything that is fighting against you. I prophesy that you will rejoice again, yes you will see the face of the Lord again! You will smile again because He loves you more than anyone else here on earth. There is no weapon fashioned against you that will prosper.

Today you can vocalize your call on Him. The Psalmist continues and says in **Psalms 22:26 "The meek shall eat and be satisfied: they shall praise the Lord that seek him: your heart shall live for ever."**

He wants to satisfy you with good things. He wants you to go through life with joy, not pains, depression, lack and other things. He wants you satisfied. As you seek His face, give Him praise! Praise is powerful and it breaks down the strongest of walls. Any stronghold that stood against you will fall as you praise the Lord.

I pray for you today that you find strength to call on Him. If you were giving up, I pray that hope swells inside of you again. Your season has come and as you praise Him, your answer is here.

DECLARATION

I praise you Lord for when I called you heard me. Thank you for showing me your face and my situation is changing as a result.

Other books by Charles Magaiza *Snr*

21 Days of fasting & Prayer- Words to Power Your Fasting Season

Detox Your Spirit- 40 Day Devotion to change your life

7 Days of Fasting & Prayer- Words to Power your Fasting Season

3 Days of Fasting & Prayer

Fasting & Prayer- Unlocking the Door to Deeper Spirituality

I have to pray but why is it so hard?

31 Day Devotional

Secrets to Answered Prayer

Your Pregnancy Devotional

Into His Presence

No Limits

Breaking the Invisible Barriers

Overcoming Grief Through Prayer

Shake It Off

Breaking the Uncle Laban Effect

From the Shepherd's Desk Devotional (Vol 1) 366 Day Devotional

Visit our author page on amazon on www.amazon.com/author/cmagaiza

www.ingramcontent.com/pod-product-compliance
Lightning Source LLC
Chambersburg PA
CBHW060616030426
42337CB00018B/3078